Ready? Set? Engage!

A Field Guide for Employees to Create Their Own Culture of Participation and Implement Innovative Ideas

Also by Michael McCarthy
*How to Engage, Involve, and Motivate Employees: Building a Culture of Lean
Leadership with Two-Way Commitment and Communication*
(with Janis Allen)
Sustain Your Gains: The People Side of Lean-Six Sigma
You Made My Day: Creating Co-Worker Recognition and Relationships
(with Janis Allen)
The Noah Option (political thriller)
The Rainbow Option (political thriller)

Also by Janis Allen
*How to Engage, Involve, and Motivate Employees: Building a Culture of Lean
Leadership with Two-Way Commitment and Communication*
(with Michael McCarthy)
World War II Veterans of Western North Carolina (history)
Stories from a Sandy Mush Girl (memoir)
You Made My Day: Creating Co-Worker Recognition and Relationships
(with Michael McCarthy)
Team Up!
*I Saw What You Did and I Know Who You Are: Bloopers, Blunders, and Success
Stories in Giving and Receiving Positive Recognition*
Performance Teams: Creating the Feedback Loop

Ready? Set? Engage!
A Field Guide for Employees to Create Their Own Culture of Participation and Implement Innovative Ideas

By
Michael McCarthy and Janis Allen

Routledge
Taylor & Francis Group
A PRODUCTIVITY PRESS BOOK

Routledge
Taylor & Francis Group
6000 Broken Sound Parkway NW, Suite 300
Boca Raton, FL 33487-2742

© 2018 by Taylor & Francis Group, LLC
Routledge is an imprint of Taylor & Francis Group, an Informa business

No claim to original U.S. Government works

Printed on acid-free paper

International Standard Book Number-13: 978-1-138-06892-6 (Paperback)

International Standard Book Number-13: 978-1-138-57544-8 (Hardback)

International Standard Book Number-13: 978-1-315-15753-5 (eBook)

Visit the Taylor & Francis Web site at
http://www.taylorandfrancis.com

and the Productivity Press Web site at
www.productivitypress.com

Printed and bound in the United States of America by Sheridan

Dedicated to
Russell Justice
who, for forty-plus years, has been making places work
better and making them better places to work.

Mike and Janis
July 2017

Contents

"Make This Place Work Better and Make It a Better Place to Work"

It's much easier to just do one of those; to do both at the same time is the challenge. Some organizations set out to "improve employee satisfaction" (make this a better place to work). That can be done, but it's far from sufficient.

Making the place work better will in some ways make it a better place to work (less frustration from waste, late deliveries, etc.), but not nearly enough.

Purposeful attention must be given to "making business easy" for the employees, customers, and suppliers.

Russell Justice
Senior Associate, Eastman Chemical Company (retired)
Founding Partner, The Transformation Network

Why Read This Book?

You've heard about "engagement" at work. You want to stop talking and get started. This is the book for you. It's a step-by-step "how-to" guide. Like instructions for "assembly required" projects, this book takes you one step at a time into creating a project that makes your work easier, better, and more satisfying.

Other books on engagement are for supervisors. This is for YOU. YOU are the person who does the work. YOU make the product or deliver the service to customers. As an employee, YOU are the closest to the process.

You may have seen many programs come and go. You might understandably be skeptical of new "programs," big announcements, training workshops, logos, surveys, and other hullabaloo. This is not a program, it's a set of assembly instructions with 5 steps:

1. **FIND**
2. **IDEAS**
3. **TEST**
4. **RECOGNIZE**
5. **SHARE**

The project you'll assemble is something you and/or your co-workers will pick. It will be a project you think *makes it easier to do your job.*

Projects PULL people, and this book will PULL you and your ideas into making your work better and making your workplace better.

Michael McCarthy and Janis Allen

P.S. This book is a companion to *How to Engage, Involve, and Motivate Employees*, which is a book for supervisors. The steps to engagement are the same; the wording is different, because this book is addressed to YOU, the person on the front line.

Ready? Set? Engage!

5-Step Method: Ready? Set? Engage!

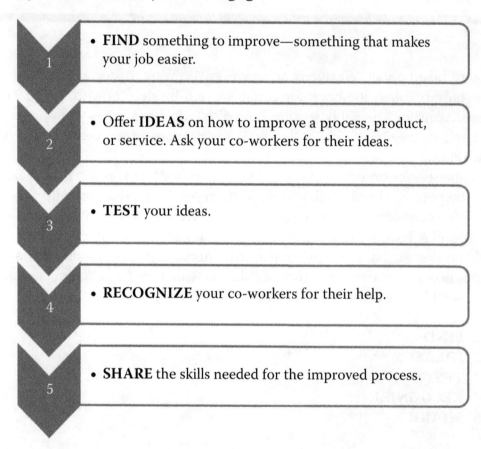

1
- **FIND** something to improve—something that makes your job easier.

2
- Offer **IDEAS** on how to improve a process, product, or service. Ask your co-workers for their ideas.

3
- **TEST** your ideas.

4
- **RECOGNIZE** your co-workers for their help.

5
- **SHARE** the skills needed for the improved process.

Introduction

Engagement: What Is It and Why Do It?

Key Points

    A. **What Is Engagement? It's Working on Projects; It's Teamwork.**
    B. **Why Engage? To Make a Difference Using Your Experience and Ideas.**
    C. **Learn from the Ideas of Your Co-Workers.**

Projects PULL People

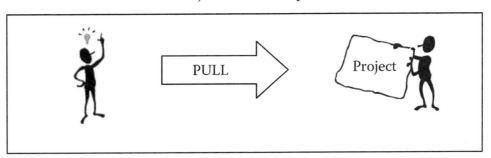

A. What Is Engagement? It's Working on Projects; It's Teamwork

When we're part of a team, we like to see our team win. Think of a time when you were in a club at school or playing a team sport. You had a role to play. It was important to play that role. Playing that position helped the team accomplish a goal. You were needed. You counted. You made a difference. That's engagement!

Pick a project that PULLS you in because it affects you directly or because you have an idea you're itching to try out. You'll look forward to making your work easier or making customers prefer your product or service.

In the table below, jot down an idea you've been wanting to suggest or test—something that will make your work process easier, or solve a problem.

The part of the work process I'd like to make easier:
_____
Solution ideas I'd like to test:
1.
2.
3.

When you're ready, volunteer to test one of the ideas you listed above. Tell your supervisor about it.

If you need help to perform the test, ask one or more of your co-workers to help you. This is how a team gets started. It might be a team of two!

How engagement "snowballs" into a team

Think of a time when you were on a team or in a club at school: the basketball or soccer team, the yearbook staff, the photography club, or Future Farmers of America. How did you feel when your team played well, or your club's project succeeded? That's how you'll feel when you're part of a team that runs a successful project at work!.

B. Why Engage? To Make a Difference Using Your Experience and Ideas

At a manufacturing plant for cathode ray tubes, moisture was found inside some of the tubes, causing quality problems. Supervisors tried unsuccessfully to find the cause of the moisture. Engineers couldn't figure it out.

When a supervisor mentioned it to one of his machine operators, the operator said, "I know what's causing it. Every once in a while, I notice an excess of moisture in the CO_2 line, and I purge it to get rid of the moisture."

The supervisor asked, "Why didn't you say something?"

The operator replied, "No one ever asked me." Then he showed all the other operators how to purge the line.

Contrast that story with this one. On a snowy day at Preston Trucking (one of Mike's clients), a driver was unable to make his scheduled deliveries in the large truck. He went home, put chains on the tires of his personal pickup truck, came to the terminal, loaded the freight into his pickup, and delivered it.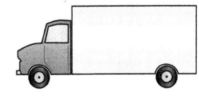

In this example, he felt that he was on the customer's team. So when the snow brought the big trucks to a halt, this driver was quick to think of a way to get those needed supplies to his customers.

He was <u>engaged</u> with his customers. He knew them and knew they needed their supplies that day.

When you get to use your own ideas, you get to use your experience and expertise to make a difference. That driver's customer might have had to send employees home without pay if they didn't get that delivery of supplies for their production that day. That driver made a difference to people's paychecks.

Not all of our ideas will get used. A batting average of .300 in major league baseball is considered excellent. Only the top 15 players in the MLB hit .310 or above last year. But that means these top players strike out seven out of ten of their times at bat. So, boldly "step up to the plate" and suggest your idea. Suggest a way to test your idea. If you strike out, don't quit. When you think of another idea, step up to the plate again.

Here's how:

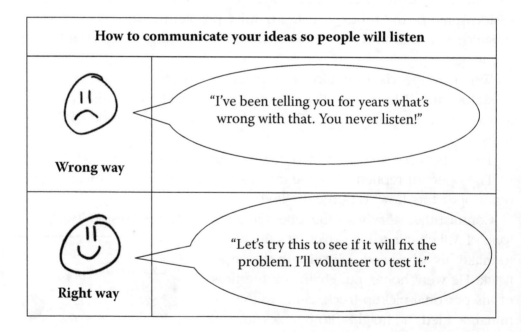

Notice that the right way is to suggest what you WANT TO DO rather than complain about how things are. When 2016 MVP Mike Trout of the Los Angeles Angels steps up to the plate, he isn't complaining about his last strikeout. He's ready to test himself against the next pitch. So when you get an idea, think, "Batter up!"

Engagement WD-40 Tip #1

Suggest your idea
and a way to test your idea.

Use Engagement WD-40:
It keeps everything moving
freely!

C. Learn from the Ideas of Your Co-Workers

Getting involved in projects gives us a chance to discuss ideas with our co-workers as we work to improve how we do our work.

Janis' example:

> *When I began working on a new book, I asked my colleague, Greg, to read my first chapter and give me his feedback. He returned it with a suggestion to add "mileposts" (sub-headings within each chapter) to separate the ideas and give my readers a clue about what was coming, as well as some "breathing" space.*

> *My reaction was, "Why didn't I think of that?" I've been writing books for years. I should've already been doing that. To be honest, I was a bit embarrassed that I had to hear this from Greg. But thankful! I added those "mileposts" to every chapter, and still do. In fact, you'll see one at the top of this section. (Aren't you glad?)* ☺

> *So often, we become so involved in the "innards" of our work that we forget to take a step back and consider methods that would make it easier for the customers who use our product or service. That good idea came because I asked a colleague for his ideas. I would hate to have missed that one!*

Think of a time when you've heard an idea from a co-worker that made your work easier or made your product or service better. Using the form that follows, jot it down and then go tell that person that you value it! (You have permission to copy the form.)

Thumbs Up to _____

Your idea of _____

made work easier because

_____

My thanks to you!

Signed: _____

You might just copy this form, complete it, and give it to that co-worker. This will make his or her day! (Be sure to sign it. That will make it extra valuable.)

	QUIZ (answers on next page)
1.	Not all _____ will get used.
2.	Suggest what you _____ rather than complain about how things are.
3.	Suggest how to _____ your idea, then _____ to perform the test.

Summary Checklist

☐ **Start an Improvement Project. Recruit a Team If Needed.**
☐ **Use Your Experience and Ideas to Make Suggestions.**
☐ **Learn from the Ideas of Your Co-Workers.**

Answers to QUIZ	
1.	ideas
2.	want to do
3.	test … volunteer

Authors

 **Michael McCarthy** has worked with teams, supervisors, and top executives as a process/performance improvement consultant, lean trainer/coach, and curriculum designer. As senior consultant with Aubrey Daniels International, his clients included Preston Trucking (a case study in the book *A Great Place to Work*), 3M, Georgia Power, Department of the Army, Ford Motor Credit, Emerson Electronics and Space Division, Fireman's Fund Insurance, and Black & Decker. Following the success of his book *Sustain Your Gains: The People Side of Lean-Six Sigma*, Mike was a keynote speaker for the European Behavior-Based Safety Conference in Bologna, Italy.

 **Janis Allen** has been an HR manager for a major textile manufacturer, a performance consultant, and vice president of operations for Aubrey Daniels International. She has owned Performance Leadership Consulting since 1991. She created the book *Performance Teams*, a process that combined Quality Circles with Performance Management for Xerox Refurbishing and Xerox Distribution. Some of her clients have included BMW Manufacturing, 3M, Philadelphia Electric, Blue Cross and Blue Shield, Wisconsin Gas, International Paper, and the New York Department of Motor Vehicles. Janis was a keynote speaker for the National Association for Employee Recognition. Her earlier book on recognition, *I Saw What You Did and I Know Who You Are*, was used by Delta Airlines. She and her husband (and co-author) Michael McCarthy wrote *You Made My Day: Creating Co-Worker Recognition and Relationships* and *How to Engage, Involve, and Motivate Employees*. Janis and Mike live in the Blue Ridge Mountains of North Carolina.

Step 1: FIND Something to Improve—Something That Makes Your Job Easier

Step 1	• **FIND** something to improve—something that makes your job easier.
Step 2	• Offer **IDEAS** to improve a process, product, or service. Ask your co-workers for their ideas.
Step 3	• **TEST** your ideas.
Step 4	• **RECOGNIZE** your co-workers for their help.
Step 5	• **SHARE** the skills needed for the improved process.

Step 1

- **FIND** something to improve—something that makes your job easier.

Key Points

A. **Go See for Yourself.**
B. **Go See How Your Customer (Internal or External) Uses Your Stuff.**
C. **The Project to Make Your Work Easier Is Likely Right under Your Nose, Annoying You Every Day. You Can Put Your Energy into Permanently Fixing That Annoying Problem, Rather Than Being Annoyed by It Daily.**

A. Go See for Yourself

Take a step back and look at your work as an observer, not the one doing the work. There are several ways you can do this.

1. If someone else does the same job you do, watch him or her. Take notes. Look for extra time spent "walking away" from the work area to get stuff, delays, or anything slowing that person down.
2. If you can't watch someone else do the same job you do, ask someone to watch you do the work. Ask that person to make a note of anything that slows you down or makes you wait. A person not familiar with the work is better, because he or she will notice things that you wouldn't. Ask that person for ideas to make the work easier.
3. Video someone (or a team) doing the work. All you need is someone to be your camera-person (or a tripod to aim the phone at the work area). Tip: Have two people watch the video and write down anything that would make it easier.

	Engagement WD-40 Tip #2
	Write each step of your work process on a separate index card or sticky note. This helps you keep the steps separate when you analyze your process. Then you can ask, "What if … ?"
Use Engagement WD-40: It keeps everything moving freely!	This allows you to experiment with rearranging steps later. Ask, "Would doing the steps in a different sequence make it easier … ?"

B. Go See How Your Customer (Internal or External) Uses Your Stuff

You'll remember the story of the truck driver who had an idea for delivering his customers' orders when the large trucks couldn't go in the snow. He saw his customers face-to-face, and knew how important deliveries were to them. That's the nature of "delivering": you get to see how your customers use your stuff. But you can find opportunities to meet your customers and see *how* they use your products or services, even if you don't normally meet them. How?

■ Ask your supervisor for the opportunity to visit your customer. This could be the customer who buys your company's products or services, or it could be the next department over, the person or people who uses your stuff: information, parts, or data. They are both your customers.

■ When you get to your customer's workplace, ask your customers to show you how they use the product or parts they get from you. Not just tell, but *show*. This will give you ideas for improvements. Here are some examples:

1. 3M: The Invention of Masking Tape

   In the early 1920s, 3M manufactured and sold abrasives. One afternoon, 3M employee Dick Drew wanted to test a new batch of sandpaper, so he visited an auto body shop in St. Paul, Minnesota. When he entered the shop, he heard a group of workers cursing vehemently. He asked about the problem. Two-tone cars were popular then, but it required workers to mask parts of the auto body using a combination of heavy adhesive tape and butcher paper. After the paint dried, workers removed the tape—and often peeled away part of the new paint. Then they had to do it over.

   Drew watched as the workers began to touch up the flawed paint. He could have seen this as an opportunity to sell more sandpaper, but realized that what the customer really needed was a tape with a less sticky adhesive. Drew also realized that 3M already had several of the elements of tape-making. Sandpaper required a backing, an adhesive, and an abrasive mineral. Hold the abrasive and you have adhesive tape.

   Drew took his idea back to the lab and began testing for the right combination of materials to create what would become the world's first masking tape. And the rest is history. History that began by seeing the customers' problems in person.

   https://en.wikipedia.org/wiki/Masking_tape

2. UPS: The Invention of "Big Brown"

   UPS' trademark color (and I do mean trademarked, they did so in 1998 to keep other delivery companies from using brown as their color) was developed when Charlie Soderstrom joined the company in 1916, nine years after the company was founded. As UPS began using trucks instead of horse-drawn vans, founder James E. Casey wanted to paint them yellow. However, Soderstrom pointed out that yellow would be impossible to keep clean, and suggested a shade of brown similar to Pullman rail cars, as the color "reflected class, elegance, and professionalism—and dirt is less visible on brown uniforms and vehicles," according to UPS. UPS has been "big brown" ever since.

   UPS Big Brown by Kate Smith

   http://www.sensationalcolor.com/brand-trademark-colors/ups-brown-1239#.WQtQKvkrIrg

Going to visit customers lets us see for ourselves. Which external or internal customer (department that receives and uses your parts or data) would you like to visit? Ask to *see* how the customer uses your data, products, or parts. *Seeing* (not just hearing about) the way the customer uses your stuff will give you ideas about how to make it better and easier for them.

Jot down your ideas below and take this as a request to your supervisor. You might even ask your supervisor to go with you.

A customer I would like to visit to see how they use our "stuff" (product or service):	Possible improvements to us and the customers (including making it easier to use our products, less re-work, fewer returns):
	1.
	2.
	3.
	4.
	5.

After you see what the customer is doing, ideas will pop into your head for making it easier to use your product.

C. The Project to Make Your Work Easier Is Likely Right under Your Nose, Annoying You Every Day. You Can Put Your Energy into Permanently Fixing That Annoying Problem, Rather than Being Annoyed by It Daily

1. Clean and Lean

In a YouTube Lean video posted by Truline Industries titled "Speed Cleaning," they show a great example of some small extra work steps that can annoy you every day. In the video, a maintenance man walks behind a floor scrubbing machine, following the yellow line marking the outer edge of the safe walking zone. A small plastic pitcher beside a computer numerical control (CNC) machine is on the yellow line, blocking the floor scrubber. A tube feeds oil drippings into the plastic pitcher, to collect the oil before it gets on the floor.

The operator has to

a. STOP the scrubber
b. MOVE the pitcher
c. RESUME cleaning with the scrubber, then
d. STOP the scrubber again, then
e. REPLACE the pitcher under the oil tube, and
f. RESUME cleaning with the scrubber

That's six extra steps just to move past a two-and-a-half foot distance that normally would be cleaned in six seconds or so, with no stops and no extra steps. Since the floors probably have to be kept clean daily for safety reasons, this is likely a daily ANNOYANCE for the scrubber operator.

Practice seeing for yourself by watching this video. Here's the link: https://youtu.be/0FyDdTb8zIk?t=11

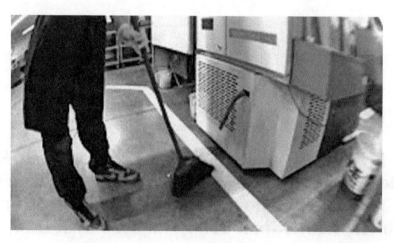

More on this story later …

Big Ears and Big Eyes

Paul Akers, the "2 Second Lean" guy, quotes Japanese Lean expert Ochio Shugo: "Good leaders need big ears and big eyes!"
   Why?

- Big ears to **HEAR** ideas or things to improve
- Big eyes to **SEE** things to improve

Look for things to improve: a checklist

- ☐ <u>What</u> slows you down?
- ☐ <u>What</u> gets in your way?
- ☐ <u>When</u> does something go wrong?
- ☐ <u>Where</u> are the bottlenecks?
- ☐ <u>Where</u> do I get frustrated because I can't get the work done?
- ☐ <u>Where</u> are people waiting for parts, information, or tools?
- ☐ <u>What</u> are our customers unhappy/complaining about?
- ☐ <u>What</u> else are our customers asking for?

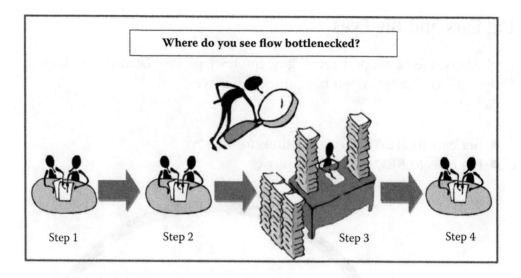

Walk the floor following the process, to SEE where the flow slows down. You'll SEE opportunities to improve your process.

QUIZ (answers on next page)	
1.	Go see for_____ .
2.	Go see your_____ (internal or external).
3.	The project to make your work easier is likely right under your nose, _____ you every day.

Answers to QUIZ	
1.	yourself
2.	customer
3.	annoying

Summary Checklist

☐ **Go See for Yourself.**

☐ **Go See How Your Customer (Internal or External) Uses Your Stuff.**

☐ **Find the Project to Make Your Work Easier. It's Likely Right under Your Nose, Annoying You Every Day.**

☐ **Find a Way to Permanently Fix That Annoying Problem, Rather Than Being Annoyed by It Daily.**

Step 2: Offer IDEAS On How to Improve a Process, Product, or Service. Ask Your Co-Workers for Their Ideas

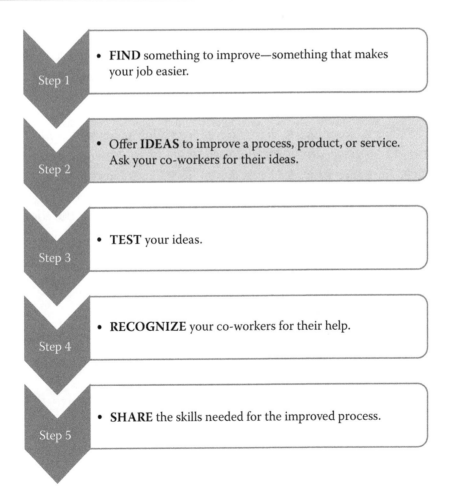

Step 1
- **FIND** something to improve—something that makes your job easier.

Step 2
- Offer **IDEAS** to improve a process, product, or service. Ask your co-workers for their ideas.

Step 3
- **TEST** your ideas.

Step 4
- **RECOGNIZE** your co-workers for their help.

Step 5
- **SHARE** the skills needed for the improved process.

> • Offer **IDEAS** to improve a process, product, or service. Ask your co-workers for their ideas.

Step 2

Key Points

A. **Brainstorm to Get Improvement Ideas.**
B. **Ask, "What Would Make the Process Easier or Simpler?"**
C. **"Play" with Ideas. Ask, "<u>What If</u> We Did It This Way?"**
D. **Volunteer to Test Your Idea.**

A. Brainstorm to Get Improvement Ideas

Brainstorming* is a quick way to generate a large number of ideas. Anyone can start a spontaneous in-the-work-area brainstorm. Simply ask for a lot of ideas on a *specific* topic.

> You: *"What are some ideas to prevent these rough spots on the filler neck?"*
> Co-worker: *"If we welded from the inside, the outside would stay smooth."*
> You: *"That's a new idea. Let's test it."*

Record *all* ideas with no judgment. It's important to write the ideas down so that the person who offered the idea knows that the idea won't fall into a black hole and get ignored.

■ Write on a note pad, or
■ Write on a flip chart, or
■ Ask co-workers to write down their own ideas on sticky notes and stick them on the flip chart for all to see, or

---

* Check out Appendix II for complete guidelines on brainstorming.

■ Post your specific questions at the place where you want the improvements. Ask your co-workers to write their ideas on sticky notes and stick them on your sheet. After four or five days, take a look at the ideas and move to Step 3—Testing.

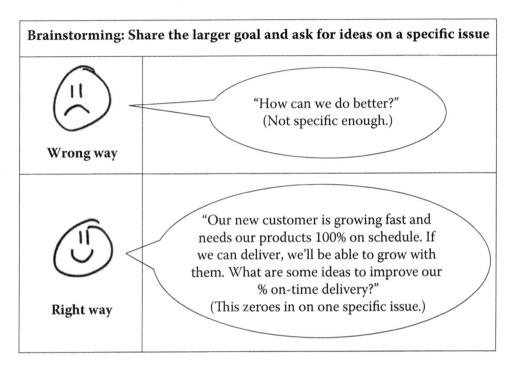

Brainstorming: Share the larger goal and ask for ideas on a specific issue

Wrong way — "How can we do better?" (Not specific enough.)

Right way — "Our new customer is growing fast and needs our products 100% on schedule. If we can deliver, we'll be able to grow with them. What are some ideas to improve our % on-time delivery?" (This zeroes in on one specific issue.)

How to react and recognize brainstormed ideas

Rephrase and allow your co-worker to explain further, or correct you if needed:

"So your idea is to _____, is that right?"

Then say, "That might work to increase/decrease/fix _____,"

And, "How can we test it?"

B. Ask, "What Would Make the Process Easier or Simpler?"

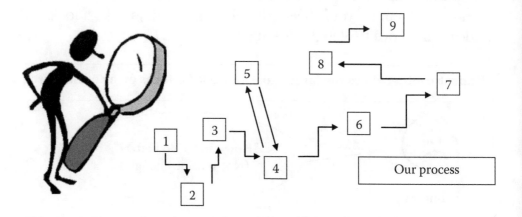

Look at the steps in our process and the time they take. What are your ideas to

- Reduce the time
- Eliminate a step
- Make a step easier to do
- Make a step safer to do
- Change the process to make a good product the first time
- Reduce the amount of walking needed to do the task
- Balance the workload among employees so that work-in-process does not pile up at one work station, or that no team member has to "strain" to keep up
- Eliminate the stopping and starting of the work flow

C. Play with Ideas: Ask, "What if We Did It This Way?"

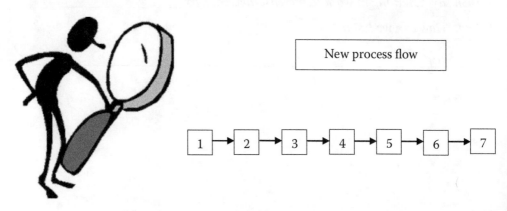

Truline Industries "Speed Cleaning," part two:
https://youtu.be/0FyDdTb8zIk?t=11

Next in the video, we see the solution (Step 2 and Step 3 in the 5-Step Method in this book.) **Step 2: Offer a SPECIFIC idea**. They have an idea to build a shelf to hold the pitcher behind the yellow line, and reroute the oil overflow tube into the pitcher at the new location. **Step 3: Test the idea.** They test the idea. It works. They even improve on the idea by routing a second oil overflow tube into the same pitcher. Now there is only one pitcher to drain, instead of two. Fewer = less work = easier job! They have eliminated six steps that annoyed this operator daily.

https://youtu.be/0FyDdTb8zIk

In this lean speed cleaning video, someone saw that the process STOPPED, the operator removed an obstacle, and then STARTED again. They brainstormed ideas, then tested one: the idea of a shelf to hold the pitcher away from the path of the cleaning machine. It worked!

	**Engagement WD-40 Tip #3** Think of what you WANT to happen (your solution idea) and then *ask* to try out your idea.
Use Engagement WD-40: It keeps everything moving freely!	You: "I'd like to re-position the plastic pitcher to get it out of the walking path. OK if I try it?" Co-worker: "OK, give it a try and let me know how it works."

D. Volunteer to Test Your Idea

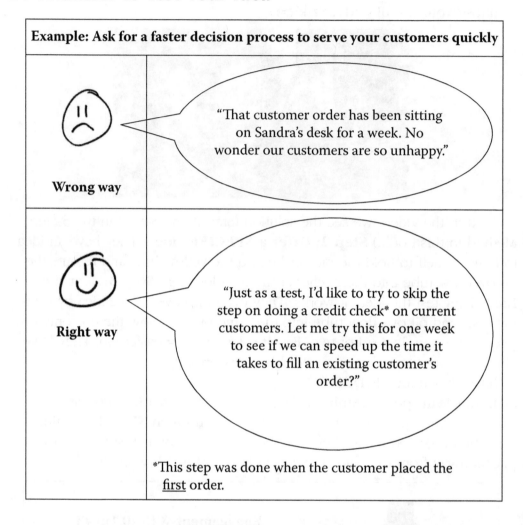

Example: Ask for a faster decision process to serve your customers quickly

Wrong way

"That customer order has been sitting on Sandra's desk for a week. No wonder our customers are so unhappy."

Right way

"Just as a test, I'd like to try to skip the step on doing a credit check* on current customers. Let me try this for one week to see if we can speed up the time it takes to fill an existing customer's order?"

*This step was done when the customer placed the <u>first</u> order.

You'll have ideas for solutions that you want to take to others (your supervisor or your co-workers). Phrase your ideas as solutions, not criticisms or details about the current process. Here's a "prop" to help you.

"Here's an idea I'd like to try:"

Make a copy of this light bulb (or draw one) and write your idea inside it. Take it with you when you suggest your idea to your co-worker. It will bring a little smile.

Use Engagement WD-40:
It keeps everything moving
freely!

Engagement WD-40 Tip #4

Ask your co-workers for new ideas to make the work easier.
Test their ideas.
Then recognize them for their help.

Pinch point warning #1:
Criticizing and blaming will shut down any willingness to try something new.
You: "This process is terrible!"
Co-worker: "Don't blame me. We were told we have to do it this way."

Avoid starting conversations like this one. Look for improvement ideas!

QUIZ (answers on next page)	
1.	Asking, "_____ _____ we did it this way?" leads to new ideas and "playing" with possible improvement ideas.
2.	Think of what you _____ to happen (solution idea) and _____ to try it out.

Answers to QUIZ	
1.	What if
2.	want ... volunteer

Summary Checklist

☐ **Brainstorm to Get Improvement Ideas.**
☐ **Ask, "What Would Make the Process Easier or Simpler?"**
☐ **Ask, "<u>What If</u> We Did It This Way?"**
☐ **Volunteer to Test Your Idea.**

Step 3: TEST Your Ideas

Step 1	• **FIND** something to improve—something that makes your job easier.
Step 2	• Offer **IDEAS** to improve a process, product, or service. Ask your co-workers for their ideas.
Step 3	• **TEST** your ideas.
Step 4	• **RECOGNIZE** your co-workers for their help.
Step 5	• **SHARE** the skills needed for the improved process.

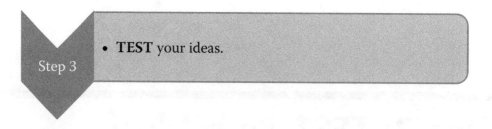

Step 3

- **TEST** your ideas.

Key Points

A. **Set Time Targets for Testing Your Ideas and Log Your Action Steps.**
B. **Share Your Project with Your Co-Workers. Ask for Their Help and Ideas to Improve.**
C. **Use a Measurement of Results as Feedback on Your Test: What Works? What Doesn't Work?**
D. **Stuck on What to Do? "Level" Your Ideas So You Can Take Action.**
E. **Arguing about What's Best? Go Test!**

A. Set Time Targets for Testing Your Ideas and Post Your Action Steps

> "(The Wright Brothers) were always thinking of the next thing to do; they didn't waste much time worrying about the past."
> ~ Charlie Taylor, mechanic for the Wright Brothers, inventors of the airplane, quoted in *The Wright Brothers*, by David McCullough

Like the Wright brothers, your next move is to think of how to test your idea. Once you decide how to test the idea, set a time target to "get 'er done." There is nothing like a deadline to get you to take action. A team project log will help you keep track of what needs to be done, and time targets for each task.

Team project log for ASSEMBLY (team)				
Date 9/22/20 now Project STAGE PARTS Measurable goal: *Reduce Cycle time 10%*				
Idea to test	Action steps	Volunteer	Start testing	Status
Store parts at point of use	1. Stage needed parts at individual work stations	Jill	June 1	Done
	2. Create 5S labels for each parts bin	Fred	June 2	Ordered label machine
	3. Calculate KanBan cards for reordering parts from suppliers	Akeem	June 4	Asked IE for calculation

Use a project log like this one to keep your action steps in front of you. Recognize team members when they complete these actions.

Feel free to copy this form:

Team project log for _____ (team)				
Date _____ Project _____ Measurable goal: _____				
Idea to test	Action step	Volunteer	Start testing	Status

B. Share Your Project with Your Co-Workers. Ask for Their Help and Ideas to Improve

Post your project log for your co-workers to see. Then ask your teammates for their ideas on SPECIFIC improvements or problems. Then add their ideas to the log and test them.

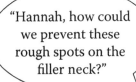
"Hannah, how could we prevent these rough spots on the filler neck?"

"Well . . . if we pressurized the inside, the welded seam would stay smooth."

	Engagement WD-40 Tip #5 **Ask specific questions** *Be Specific when you ask others for their ideas.* Being specific gives them something concrete to focus on.
Use Engagement WD-40: It keeps everything moving freely!	Not, "How can we improve?" but "How can we eliminate these burrs in the finished metal?"

Ask Co-Workers for Help with Your Project

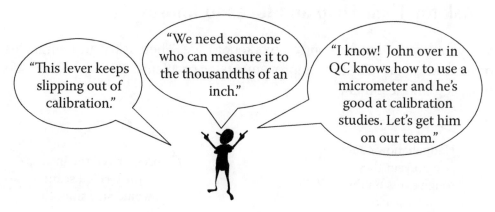

"This lever keeps slipping out of calibration."

"We need someone who can measure it to the thousandths of an inch."

"I know! John over in QC knows how to use a micrometer and he's good at calibration studies. Let's get him on our team."

When you ask for John's help, be careful not to meet his every idea with a "Yes, but ..." (a reason that it won't work). That would send the message that you don't need his ideas after all. Listen to his ideas carefully and suggest a test of his idea. Then use your measurement data to see how well John's idea works.

Pinch point warning #2
You could "pinch" off your co-workers' flow of ideas with constant criticism. Then they'll stop giving you ideas. Instead, choose ideas to test. Then pick the idea that tests the best.

C. Use a Measurement of Results as Feedback on Your Test: What Works? What Doesn't Work?

Every game a sports team plays is a kind of test. The coach has a game plan. The players have been practicing skills and moves. Test: is the game plan the right game plan? Test: are the players skilled enough on their moves? The "test results" are on the scoreboard. And the test results are there in **real time**. Game plan: working, or not working? Check the score to find out. Players: skilled enough? Not skilled enough? Check the score to find out.

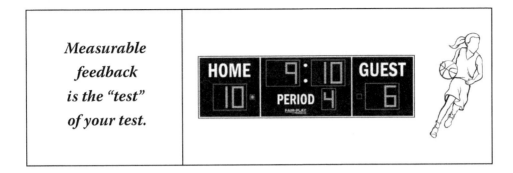

> *Measurable feedback is the "test" of your test.*

You are the "coach" of your project. You need a "score" to tell if your ideas are working or not. What should you measure for your "score?" What data do you want to see for your test? Use data that shows you how you're doing in meeting your goals. In the example graph below, you would want to track the cycle time for completing a unit. Then you would mark the 10% cycle time reduction you are hoping your improvement idea will achieve. If cycle time to complete a unit was 10 min, then 9 min would be your 10% reduction in cycle time. You want to know if your idea of stocking parts at the point of use saves the time it used to take going to the storeroom to replenish the parts you need for your work. If it does save time, the average cycle time to make a part will be quicker than it used to be (what it used to be = baseline. Compare your results to baseline to know if your idea helped or not).

In the example of cycle time, your graph might look like this:

Department X: Reduce cycle time Idea: stock parts at each work station.							
10 min	**Baseline**						
9.75 min							
9,5min							
9 min					**Goal: 10% reduction**		
Week ending	1/6 (Baseline)	1/13	1/20	1/27	2/3	2/10	2/17

The easiest way to know this is to make it visual. Graphs are an easy visual to help you and your team see if your idea is working or not. If it works, great! Ask your supervisor how to make this idea the new standard work or standard operating procedure. If it doesn't work, move on to test the next idea. This was just a test.

In this case, your idea worked because as you and your co-workers *became more practiced in using the new idea*, cycle time came down gradually to the hoped-for goal of a 10% reduction; down to 9 min. The bar graph makes it easy to see this.

What to Put on the Graph?

Ask yourself, what is the **result** that you are trying to improve? Then find a simple way to measure that result. If the result is important to the main purpose of the company, keep measuring it and keep a graph on it posted daily or weekly.

Examples:

- For a trucking/logistics company, **result**=% on-time deliveries. It's what customers pay them to do: deliver their stuff on time. Improvement **ideas** could be about how to load the trucks faster and more safely.
- For a grocery store, a goal is keeping the shelves stocked with food. It's the reason customers go there—to buy food. If the store runs out of an item, customers can't buy it. Measurable **result**=% items in stock on shelves. Improvement **ideas** could be about how to make stocking the shelves easier.
- For an online movie streaming service like Netflix, a goal is keeping the shows streaming to your television set or device. That is what the customer is paying for. Measurable **result**=% uptime of servers streaming the movies and TV shows. Improvement **ideas** could be about how to make the servers more reliable.

When Do You NOT Need a Graph?

Sometimes, you will make the call that a graph is not needed for you to know if your test idea worked or not. In the chapter for Step 2, we saw the idea of putting the plastic pitcher on a shelf so that the scrubber operator would not have the extra steps of stopping to move it. We can tell that the idea worked without using a graph. Why? Because now the scrubber operator doesn't have to stop! He keeps on moving. Mission accomplished, test idea successful. If you can see it for yourself = no graph needed.

When DO You Need a Graph?

If the measurable result is about the basic purpose of the business, then we should keep the graph posted and up to date at all times. Why? Because it shows us something the customer is paying us to do. For example, if I work for a grocery store and the grocery shelves keep getting empty, the customers will go someplace else to buy groceries. Then the store will shut down and I won't have a job! The graph is part of a "dashboard" of *measurements we need* to run our department and/or the business. Just like you need a dashboard of measurements to operate your car properly, such as fuel tank % full, engine temperature, and speed. Each of these measurements is FEEDBACK to us. They tell us when to DO something: get gas, check the engine coolant level, or slow down.

Then, like your automobile dashboard, you'll need to check it frequently. Why? The un-engaged driver (who didn't pay attention to the fuel gauge measurement) is the one walking with a fuel can.

Use data as feedback to see if your project is working

Wrong way

"We don't need to measure our results. Just do some stuff."

Right way

"This graph shows our on-time delivery for the month is 90%. Our customers want 100%. Let's look for ideas to improve our delivery process. When we test an idea, let's check the graph daily to see if on-time delivery improves above 90%."

Graphs for Project Feedback

When it's a team project, individual team members can take turns updating the graph, but discuss the data with everyone involved. Here's how your team's graph might look:

Department X: On-time delivery							
100%							Goal - - - - -
98%					Sub-goal - - - - -	- - - -	
96%				Sub-goal - - - - -			
94%			Sub-goal - - - - -				
92%		Sub-goal - - - - -					
90%	●						
Week Ending	1/6 (Baseline)	1/13	1/20	1/27	2/3	2/10	2/17

Use Engagement WD-40: It keeps everything moving freely!

Engagement WD-40 Tip #6

Graph It!

Post graphs to give you a "moving picture" of your progress. A picture is worth a thousand words.

Pinch Point Warning #3:
Keep your graphs and project logs up to date or take them down. Out-of-date graphs become wallpaper and teach everyone to *ignore* posted information.

D. Stuck about What to Do? "Level" Your Ideas So You Can Take Action

How often have you attended meeting after meeting and looked at the same ideas in the meeting minutes, just stuck there, with no action taken? Arggghhhhh!

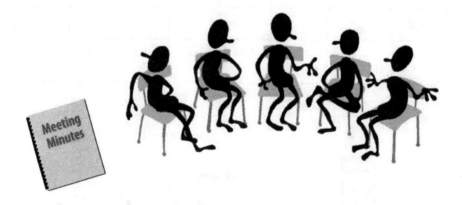

Though the ideas may be ones that the group thinks will work, they get stuck and go nowhere because there's no specific next step to DO. There's nothing *concrete* and *specific* for anyone to DO. Here's how to come up with that specific next step to get these "stuck" ideas moving: level 'em.

Leveling is sorting out ideas into three levels:

Level 1: Ideas that can be safely tested right away by just you and your co-workers. Ask your supervisor if she/he wants to be included, or just kept informed. **Action**: make a plan to test it and see if it works.

Level 2: Ideas that need approval or help from another person (outside of you, your supervisor, and any co-workers helping with the project), another department, or the customer. **Action**: Go ask that person or department for help.

Level 3: Ideas that you are not sure are Level 1 or 2. Decide what additional information you need in order to decide if it is a Level 1 or a Level 2. **Action**: Go ask someone for that information.

Leveling
Place your selected idea into one of these levels

State the idea: _____

If:	Then this idea is a:	Specific action I can take:	
I can test or implement this idea without informing or checking with anyone else (other than my supervisor and co-workers I've already discussed the idea with)	Level 1	Volunteer to test or implement the idea and write down a target date to get it done.	*Go!*
I need to check with someone else (who might be affected) before testing this idea: another person, another department, or the customer.	Level 2	Volunteer to check with the person and write down a target date to get it done.	*Need to ask others.*
I need more information before deciding whether it's Level 1 or Level 2	Level 3	Volunteer to get the information and write down a target date to get this done.	*Get info or data.*

Use Engagement WD-40: It keeps everything moving freely!

Engagement WD-40 Tip #7

Level 'Em

Level your ideas to get them "un-stuck." Level your ideas to create small, concrete steps that you can DO today.

Using leveling, you will have a small concrete step that you or another volunteer can DO today, such as contact an individual or get information. After that's done, you're ready to decide on another step.

E. Arguing about What's Best? Go Test!

How to stop disagreeing and start improving			
Possible solution that we don't have agreement on: _____ _____ _____	Suggestion for performing a test to see how well the idea will work: _____ _____ _____ _____	Or, data, information, or feedback we can gather from the customer to see if the idea will work: _____ _____ _____ _____	What we learned from *testing* or *visiting* the customer: _____ _____ _____ _____
	Who will perform this test _____ _____ by _____ (date)	Who will visit the customer _____ by _____ (date)	

Use Engagement WD-40: It keeps everything moving freely!

Engagement WD-40 Tip #8

If your team is arguing about an idea, stop and:

1. Test the idea

2. Get more facts about what causes the problem

3. Go to your customer's workplace to SEE how they're using your product or service

	QUIZ (answers on next page)
1.	Set _____ targets for _____ your ideas
2.	Share your project with your _____ and ask for their _____ and _____
3.	A graph of measurable results will tell you whether or not your idea _____
4.	Keep your logs and graphs up-to-date or _____ them _____.
5.	If stuck, _____ your ideas and then take _____
6.	If arguing, do a _____ instead.

Answers to QUIZ	
1.	time ... testing
2.	co-workers ... help ... ideas
3.	works
4.	take ... down
5.	level ... action
6.	test

Summary Checklist

☐ **Set Time Targets for Testing Your Ideas and Log Your Action Steps.**

☐ **Share Your Project with Your Co-Workers. Ask for Their Help and Ideas to Improve Further.**

☐ **Use Visual Data on GRAPHS to See If Your Test Idea Is Working or Not.**

☐ **If Stuck, Level Your Ideas and Take Action.**

☐ **Don't Argue; Go Perform a Test.**

Step 4: RECOGNIZE Your Co-Workers for Their Help

Step 1	• **FIND** something to improve—something that makes your job easier.
Step 2	• Offer **IDEAS** to improve a process, product, or service. Ask your co-workers for their ideas.
Step 3	• **TEST** your ideas.
Step 4	• **RECOGNIZE** your co-workers for their help.
Step 5	• **SHARE** the skills needed for the improved process.

Step 4

• **RECOGNIZE** your co-workers for their help.

Key Points

A. **Why Give Recognition?**
B. **What to Recognize.**
C. **How to Recognize.**
D. **Create "Show and Tell" Recognition at Work and at Home.**
E. **"Trebek 'Em!"—Three Words: "That's the Way!"**

A. Why Give Recognition?

Janis' example:

> When I was 11 years old, I cut the grass in my family's yard all by myself for the first time. I was tired and sweaty, but so proud. I did this voluntarily and it made me feel "oh, so grown-up."
>
> A family friend pulled into the driveway just as I was admiring my work. His first words out of the car were, "You missed a spot behind the shrubs." I was crushed. Why hadn't he commented about the rest of the four acres that I had mowed perfectly with so much sweat and effort? I suppose his eye was trained to look for the imperfections. But I never wanted to cut grass again.

So, the answer to the question "Why give recognition?" is simple: "Because we want people to feel appreciated and want to do it again!"

Two-Second Recognition

A smile and a two-word comment like, "Looks good!" makes us want to keep doing whatever it is that earned this positive recognition. When I encounter a cleaning person cleaning in a public restroom, I make a point to look around and, if the evidence says "clean," I make eye contact with that cleaning person, smile, and say, "Looks good."

Takes only two seconds.

> **Want somebody to feel part of the team? Recognize them for**
> **what they did.**
> **Want them to do it again?**
> **Recognize them for what they did.**

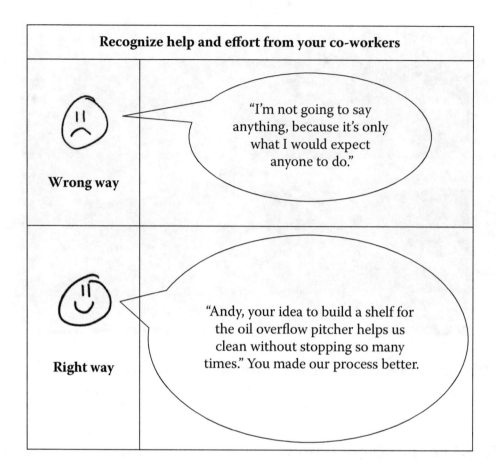

B. What to Recognize

1. As you walk through your work area, you'll see actions (even small ones) that your co-workers are doing to make your project successful. For instance, you'll SEE
   a. Someone testing an idea
   b. Someone completing an item from the project test log
   c. Someone following a new process correctly
2. As you walk through your work area, you'll HEAR
   a. Someone telling about a test she performed
   b. Someone telling about an action he did to move the project along
   c. Someone explaining a step in the new process to a co-worker

These are the things you can give the two-second comment about. Your two-second comment will show your co-workers that you *notice* and *appreciate* their effort and help.

Use Engagement WD-40:
It keeps everything
moving freely!

Engagement WD-40 Tip #9

Nice is nice. Recognition points at what people DID.

"But I always say 'Looking good' to everybody." That's being nice and we want nice. *Recognition*, however, points out what someone DID that's helpful. Just as you spray WD-40 exactly where it's needed, you "point" your recognition to exactly what your co-worker DID. "You printed the 5S labels for all the parts bins. Looking good."

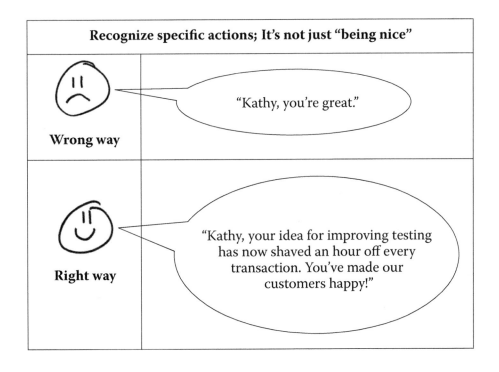

Recognize specific actions; It's not just "being nice"

Wrong way — "Kathy, you're great."

Right way — "Kathy, your idea for improving testing has now shaved an hour off every transaction. You've made our customers happy!"

C. How to Recognize

Recognition is letting someone know that you *noticed* and *appreciated* their help and ideas. Just mention that you notice what they're doing (or have done) to move the project along. Just your small, quick comment or even a non-verbal "thumbs up" can show appreciation.

Here are some examples of meaningful positive recognition that are easy to do. Just point to what your co-worker DID to help and say

1. "I appreciate your volunteering to test that idea, Dan."
2. "Lynn, your suggestion to combine two steps was a process improvement that reduced our cycle time."
3. "Matthew, we don't have to clean up oil spills here anymore, thanks to your suggestion of a pitcher to catch the overflow."
4. Nothing: try "E.P.T." Make EYE contact, POINT to the spot that has no oil on it, and give the THUMBS UP signal.

 +  **+**

5. In a note left at the location, say what you noticed and appreciated.

> Buck, you marked where your tools go. Makes it easy for me to return them to the right place. Thanks. ~ Mike

We often notice when our co-workers take actions that help us, but sometimes take them for granted. When you notice helpful actions, make a two-second comment or a silent "E.P.T."

Use Engagement WD-40: It keeps everything moving freely!

Engagement WD-40 Tip #10

Let your co-workers know that you notice and appreciate their help and effort. Make your notice noticed! How? "E. P. T."

- Eye contact

- Point to what they did

- Thumbs up sign of approval

Think of a time when you've heard an idea from a co-worker that made your work easier or made your product or service better. Using the form that follows, jot it down and then go tell that person that you value it! (You have permission to copy the form.)

You might just copy this form, complete it, and give it to that co-worker.

Thumbs Up to _____

Your idea of _____

Made my/our work easier because

_____

My thanks to you!

Signed: _____

This will make his or her day! (Be sure to sign it. That will make it extra valuable.)

 **Pinch Point Warning #4:**

When you give positive recognition, let it stand alone.

Don't follow it with "but." Example: "Noah, you gave us a good idea. But you didn't volunteer to test it." Give your positive recognition and stop. This will give your recognition time to sink in and have maximum  effect. Ask for anything else you need at a <u>different time</u>. And *no buts*! "But" erases the positive thing you just said.

D. Create "Show & Tell" Recognition at Work and at Home

Show and Tell

Use "Show and Tell" as a pause to allow for respectful recognition of a person's action or achievement. Use this pause to:

1. Tell the person you're proud of what he or she accomplished.

2. Ask, "Would you tell me/us how you did it?"

3. Then listen without commenting about how he could have done it better (that would only make him feel bad, not good). Show and Tell is just for expressing pride in achievement and nothing else.

Listen without telling the person your "better idea."

When you make Show and Tell a habit, you'll start seeing more and more things and people to be proud of. How? At the end of a tool-box meeting, ask, "Anybody got an improvement to report?" Then just listen. Sometimes just listening is the best recognition you can give a person.

Show and Tell in Everyday Life

When our former boss, Aubrey Daniels, finished a project around the house, he called out, "I need somebody!" When his wife or daughter came, he showed them the repair he'd just completed. They knew their job was to OOH and AAH and say what they liked without criticism. Why? Because they wanted him to do it again!

You can give this valuable gift to your family, and you can teach them how to give it to you. What could be better than creating a more positive atmosphere at home? Tonight at the supper table, ask your kids and spouse what they did today that they feel good about. Then just listen with all of your might! No suggestions on how they could've done it better. You'll be proud and so will they.

E. "Trebek 'Em!"—Three Words: "That's the Way!"

Trebek 'Em!
(Alex Trebek-style Recognition)

Watching Jeopardy, we appreciate Host Alex Trebek's quick, frequent, and punchy recognition comments when contestants answer correctly.
  For instance:

"That's the river."
"She's the artist."
"He's the one."

Alex keeps things moving quickly with very short comments. Useful for quick recognition of someone's ideas, even before you know if the idea can be used. For instance:

"That's an idea, Molly."
"Let's test it, Luke."
"It's a possibility, Allie."

This is a quick and easy way to say, "This is useful."

"Trebek 'Em!"

Challenge:

Write down two of your own quick "Trebeks" you can say when you see a co-worker doing something helpful:

1. _____

2. _____

	QUIZ (answers on next page)
1.	Recognition is letting someone know that you _____, and _____ something that they _____
2.	"_____" erases your recognition.
3.	E.P.T. is a quick and silent way to give recognition. It means _____, then _____ to what the person did, and then make the _____ sign.
4.	Show and Tell is when you point out someone else's achievement and then ask "_____ did you do that?" and then just _____ to her or him explain.

Answers to QUIZ	
1.	noticed ... appreciated ... did
2.	But
3.	eye contact ... point ... thumbs up
4.	How ... listen

Summary Checklist

☐ **Recognize Co-Workers When They Help You and Offer Ideas.**

☐ **Recognize Them by Letting Them Know You Notice and Appreciate Their Help and Ideas.**

☐ **Recognize with a Short Comment and/or by Pointing to What They've Done and Giving a "Thumbs Up" Sign.**

☐ **Create "Show and Tell" at Work and at Home: Ask What They're Proud of and Then Listen without Buts or Criticism.**

☐ **"Trebek 'Em" with Three Words: "That's the Way!"**

Step 5: SHARE the Skills Needed for the Improved Process

- **FIND** something to improve—something that makes your job easier.

  Step 1

- Offer **IDEAS** to improve a process, product, or service. Ask your co-workers for their ideas.

  Step 2

- **TEST** your ideas.

  Step 3

- **RECOGNIZE** your co-workers for their help.

  Step 4

- **SHARE** the skills needed for the improved process.

  Step 5

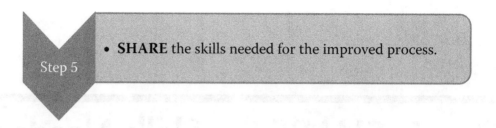

Step 5

• **SHARE** the skills needed for the improved process.

Key Points

A. **Why Share Skills for the Improved Process?**
B. **How to Share Skills.**
C. **Acquire New Skills for Yourself.**

A. Why Share Skills for the Improved Process?

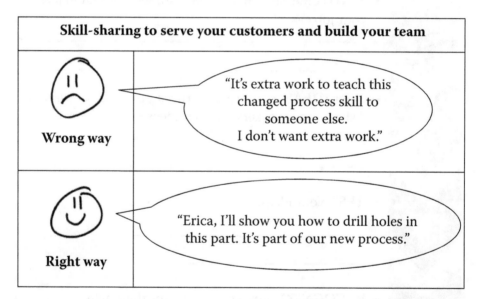

First, you want everyone to be skilled at using the new idea/process.

Second, if they aren't coached to do it the new way, they'll go back to the old way in three days or less. Then your work to find a better way is wasted.

For more on this, see *Sustain Your Gains* by Michael McCarthy at www.the5Sstore.com.

Mike's example:

Once someone told me about a shortcut I could take to get home. The next night I worked late and it was dark when I began my drive home. I drove home the old way.

Why?

1. *I had not practiced the new route and I was afraid I'd get lost in the dark.*
2. *Although the old way was longer, I knew it by heart. Everyone, including me, needs practice to get comfortable with any new process, even if they know it's better.*

> *The procedure isn't "new and improved" unless every team member*
> *is DOING it the new and improved way.*

Have you ever had to stop production and wait "because Ginger isn't here, and she's the only one who knows how to use the new process of measuring with a micrometer?" Waiting is one of the Seven Wastes of Lean Manufacturing. Cut out or reduce waiting, and you make the job easier to do. Solution? Ask Ginger to train everyone else how to use a micrometer.

Every time you share the skills of the improved process, you're improving the chances of your project's success.

>
> *Coming together is a beginning; keeping together is progress;*
> *working together is success.*
>
> ~ Henry Ford

Skill or Habit?

A skill is knowing how to do something. If you don't know how, ask some-one to show you. A skill isn't useful until it's a habit. A habit is something you do automatically, without having to think about it—like tying shoelaces. Sometimes the new process doesn't require a new skill, but doing the steps in a different sequence.

Mike's example: I use cream in my coffee. My original process was

1. Pour coffee
2. Add cream
3. Stir
4. Drink

Janis showed me an improved process:

1. Pour cream in the cup
2. Add coffee (no stirring needed)
3. Drink

I already had the skills of pouring, adding cream, and drinking. I just needed to practice the steps in the new sequence until the new process became a habit.

What skills could you share with one or more of your co-workers?

Skills-building ensures that the improved process stays improved		
A skill (or changed habit) needed for the improved process:	Co-worker(s) I could teach this skill or habit:	Date completed:

B. How to Share Skills

1. Offer to show a co-worker the new skill.
2. Pick a low-pressure time (when there isn't a delivery/production deadline).
3. Plan to teach one small part of one skill at a time. Discipline yourself to get to the bottom line quickly without unneeded background information. Translation: Don't talk him to death. SHOW him.

   EXCEPTION: SAFETY INFORMATION. Background information on safety is sometimes needed. They need to know WHY it's a safety rule to do the job in a certain way.
4. Go to the place in your work area where this skill is used for the new process.
5. Demonstrate the skill, slowly, talking through each step as you do it.
6. Ask your co-worker to practice by doing the operation "hands-on" with HER FINGERS. Ask her to talk through each step as she does it (just like you did). People learn faster with the **"talk through as you do"** method.

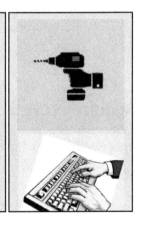

> Remember how the cops on TV tell the bad guy: "Show me your hands and step away from the body?" Your version of this for teaching skills is, "Show me your hands on the tool (or keyboard) and *I'll* step away from the work bench (or computer)."

Let the person do it. He or she will learn faster.

7. Give positive recognition to her correct attempts to demonstrate the skill ("That's it!") and all improvement ("You're doing better."). Reinforce small steps and come back later to teach another small step.

Silently recognize improvement (see E.P.T. from Step 4):

E = Eye contact

P = Point to what the person is doing

T = Thumbs up

Pinch point warning #5

When teaching and sharing skills, small steps are the keys to success. Be careful not to overwhelm your co-worker with too much to learn at one time.

C. Acquire New Skills for Yourself

The more skills you have, the more valuable you are on the job. When a new job opening comes up that pays more, and you already have the skills to do that job, then you are more likely to get that job. If you see a better-paying job opportunity in another company and you have the skills to do the job, you are more likely to get the job. More skills make you the "go-to guy" or the "go-to woman."

 *Use Engagement WD-40: It keeps everything moving freely!*	**Engagement WD-40 Tip #11** • For effective training, take your hands off the tool (or keyboard) and step away from the work table. Let your learner do the operation with her fingers. Ask your learner to "talk through it as you do it." • You watch and listen. Recognize your learner for improvement. Correct mistakes and have the learner practice again.

	QUIZ (answers on next page)
1.	It isn't "new and improved" until the team has the _____ to _____ it the "new and improved" way.
2.	Let your learner do the operation with _____ _____.
3.	Ask your learner to _____ through each step as they ____ it.
4.	The more _____ you have, the more _____ you are on the job.

Answers to QUIZ	
1.	skills ... do
2.	her fingers
3.	talk ... do
4.	skills ... valuable

Summary Checklist

☐ **Share Skills by Teaching a Co-Worker How to Do the New Process.**
☐ **Train with "Small Steps," THEIR FINGERS, and Positive Recognition.**
☐ **Ask Your Learner to Talk through the Skill as They Do It.**
☐ **Acquire New Skills for Yourself to Increase Your Own Value on the Job in the Long Run.**

The 5-Step Method in Action

Looking back to Wilbur and Orville Wright's world-changing development of the flying machine in 1903, we can see how the 5-Step Method fits how they did it:

	Ready? Set? Engage! 5-Step Method	*The Wright Brothers Perfected the Flying Machine*
Step 1	**FIND** something to improve—something that makes your job easier.	Improved on flying gliders that could only fly a short distance and fly a straight line. Found a way to make them fly further, rise, descend, and return.
Step 2	Offer **IDEAS** to improve a process, product, or service. Ask your co-workers for their ideas.	Idea: went to Kitty Hawk and used the constant wind to test ideas. Asked mechanic Charlie Taylor to build an engine lightweight enough to power an aeroplane.
Step 3	**TEST** your ideas.	Conducted test after test in Kitty Hawk. Built wind tunnel to test ideas in Dayton and added rudder, propeller, and ailerons.
Step 4	**RECOGNIZE** your co-workers for their help.	Positive comments between Wilbur and Orville when an idea worked. Used Charlie Taylor's engine and credited him with designing it.
Step 5	**SHARE** the skills the for the improved process.	The Wright Brothers taught pilots in France and the U.S. to fly their plane, so that many people could use the plane successfully.

TRULINE INDUSTRIES

How Truline's "Speed Cleaning" Video Maps to the 5-Step Method

	Ready? Set? Engage! 5-Step Method	*Lean Manufacturing* Speed Cleaning
Step 1	**FIND** something to improve—something that makes your job easier.	The floor scrubber operator has to stop to move the oil container from his path. This makes his work slower and more difficult.
Step 2	Offer **IDEAS** to improve a process, product, or service. Ask your co-workers for their ideas.	Idea: build a shelf to hold the container away from the floor. Use a co-worker's idea: feed two oil drainage tubes into the same container.
Step 3	**TEST** your ideas.	Containers placed on shelf with two oil drainage tubes feeding into it. The floor scrubber operator does not have to stop.
Step 4	**RECOGNIZE** your co-workers for their help.	Everyone who helped is thanked for their help. Some are in a YouTube video demonstrating the process improvement.
Step 5	**SHARE** the skills needed for the improved process.	The video is posted so that other scrubber operators in other plants can use the same idea to make their jobs easier and faster.

Worksheet for Your Improvement Project		
	Ready? Set? Engage! *5-Step Method*	*My Project:*
Step 1	**FIND** something to IMPROVE—something that makes your job easier.	
Step 2	Offer **IDEAS** to improve a process, product, or service. Ask your co-workers for their ideas.	
Step 3	**TEST** your ideas.	
Step 4	**RECOGNIZE** your co-workers for their help.	
Step 5	**SHARE** the skills needed for the improved process.	

Appendix I: Launch Guide: Ready? Set? Engage!

1. **FIND** something to improve—something that makes your job easier.
   - ☐ Go into the work place and watch how the work is done.
   - ☐ Go see your internal or external customers and watch how they use your product or service.
2. Offer your specific **IDEAS** to improve your process, product, or service and ask your co-workers for their ideas.
   - ☐ Ask yourself and others, "What would make our process easier or simpler?"
   - ☐ "Play" with ideas. Ask, "What if we did it this way?"
   - ☐ Volunteer to test your idea.
3. **TEST** your ideas.
   - ☐ Set time targets for testing your ideas.
   - ☐ Share your results with your co-workers and ask for their ideas to improve.
   - ☐ "Level" your ideas so that you can take action immediately.
4. **RECOGNIZE** your co-workers for their help.
   - ☐ Make positive comments or give "thumbs up" for helpful actions.
   - ☐ Do "show and tell" for yourself and co-workers for successful projects.
   - ☐ "Trebek 'em!" ... three words: "That's the way!"
5. **SHARE** the skills needed for the improved process.
   - ☐ Coach your co-workers on how to do work the new way.
   - ☐ Train a co-worker to do this in small steps.
   - ☐ Ask the learner to "talk through" the steps as they do them.
   - ☐ Acquire new skills for yourself.

Appendix II: Checklist for Successful Brainstorming

Checklist for successful brainstorming

(Brainstorming means generating lots of ideas for possible testing.)

1. Brainstorming can best be done <u>where</u> the work is done. Why? Because looking at the actual work flow (and tools and materials) will give you ideas.

2. Go to where the work is done. Take a tabletop easel pad or legal pad and sticky notes. Look at the actual part of the process that you want to make easier.

3. Write your brainstorming **<u>topic</u>** as a "how to" at the top of a tabletop flip chart (or legal pad). "How to make it easier to clean the floor."

4. Ask yourself and co-workers for ideas: "How can we improve/solve this?"

5. You and the others jot down **all** ideas on sticky notes (this is very important). All ideas are welcome, even "stupid" ideas. No criticism allowed from anyone in the group. Reason? Some of the greatest ideas in history sounded stupid *at the time*. "You Wright brothers think you can fly like a bird? That's crazy!"

6. You and your co-workers **pick** ideas to test first (see Appendix III). Circle the top 1-3 ideas picked. Don't strike through ideas in an effort to pare down the list before picking. Just pick three you think might work and plan ways to test them.

7. When ideas are mentioned which aren't directly related to this issue, put them on a separate sheet named "the parking lot." Save it and come back to it later when you're ready to deal with it as a separate issue.

Appendix III: Pick Ideas to Test

Stick up the sticky notes (with the brainstormed ideas) on an easel or on a wall. Ask your team to look at the brainstormed ideas. Tell them they each have three "T"s (for "test"). Ask each to write a "T" next to the ideas they want to test first. They can use all three of their "T"s on one idea, or two "T"s on one idea and the other on a different one, or spread their three "T"s to three different ideas. Circle the three ideas that get the most "T"s.

Idea #1	Idea #2	Idea #3	Idea #4	Idea #5
T T T	T	T T T T	T T	T T T

When you've picked your three ideas, level them.

Level the Ideas so Decisions Can Be Made and/or Actions Can Be Taken Immediately

Leveling is the process to determine whether the ideas

1. *Can be tested right away without first getting approvals (Level 1)*
2. *Need approval from someone else who would be affected (Level 2)*
3. *Need more information to determine whether they are Level 1, 2, or 3*

Leveling: Which level is this idea?			
State the idea: _____			
If:	**Then this idea is a:**	**Specific action I can take:**	
I can test or implement this idea without informing or checking with anyone else (other than my supervisor and co-workers I've already discussed the idea with)	**Level 1**	Volunteer to test or implement the idea and write down a target date to get it done.	*Go test!*
I need to check with someone else (who might be affected) before testing this idea. Another person, another department, or the customer.	**Level 2**	Volunteer to check with the person and write down a target date to get it done.	*Go ask others.*
I need more information before deciding whether it's Level 1 or Level 2.	**Level 3**	Volunteer to get the information and write down a target date to get this done.	32 44 39 41 *Go get info or data.*

Appendix IV: Tips for Teamwork

Key Points

A. **How to Build Teamwork**
B. **Don't "Water the Whiners"**

A. Tips for How to Build Teamwork

Tip: Ask a co-worker for help or ideas.
Tip: Ignore any sarcastic or negative comments.
Tip: Thank co-workers for their help and ideas. Tell the supervisor or team leader how they helped.

If the person you ask for help, or the person you invite to work with you, is not interested, respect their wishes. Don't spend a lot of time and energy trying to "convince" them. At another time, you may get help by asking for her ideas on another specific issue, listening carefully to her ideas if she's ready to offer them, and testing one of her ideas. It may take several times for her to accept your interest.

What if ... you thank the person and give her or him credit by telling the supervisor about their contributions, and the person doesn't like it? Stop! Not everybody wants recognition for their efforts. Respect his or her wishes.

TIPS TO BUILD TEAMWORK	IF THIS DOESN'T WORK
Ask a co-worker for help or ideas.	Wait for the next improvement situation, then ask again.
Ignore any sarcastic or negative comments.	Find other people to brainstorm project ideas with.
Thank co-workers for their help and ideas. "Brag" to the supervisor or team leader about how they helped.	If they tell you they don't like this, stop.

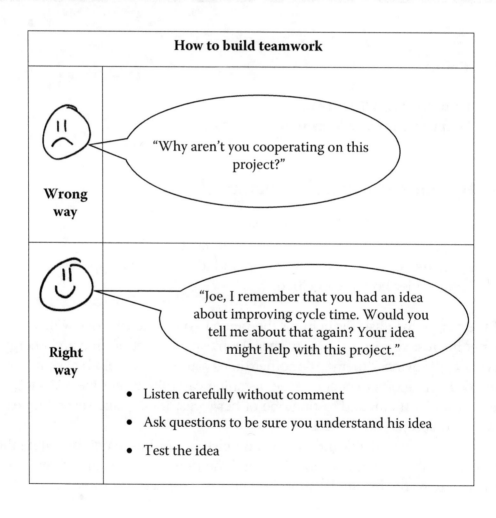

How to build teamwork

Wrong way

"Why aren't you cooperating on this project?"

Right way

"Joe, I remember that you had an idea about improving cycle time. Would you tell me about that again? Your idea might help with this project."

- Listen carefully without comment
- Ask questions to be sure you understand his idea
- Test the idea

B. Don't "Water the Whiners"

If your co-worker makes a negative comment while you're working on your project, try to ignore it and keep moving. If he continues, pay no attention and find other helpful co-workers for your projects.

> Tip: Whiners are like weeds: they always pop up.
>
> Trying to convince a whiner is like watering a weed. It only grows worse!

Just as weeds choke out a garden, whiners will choke out your ideas. The best thing you can do is ignore the whining and spend your time with co-workers who want to be helpful and make the work easier and better.

> Tip: Ignore any negative or sarcastic comments.

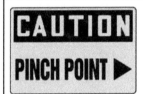

Pinch point warning #6:

Don't "water the whiners" by listening to them.

Listening to them is like watering a weed. Trying to convince them (by giving your attention) is like watering a weed. It only grows worse. Ignore them and spend time with the people who *want* to offer ideas and who *want* to make the work easier and better.

Appendix V: Recognition

Tips For Positive Recognition

4 Tips to make your recognition effective

- Be specific

> Not just, "You do a good job," but, "You caught that error. You saved time for us."

- Let your recognition stand alone. Don't ask for something more. Don't add a criticism.

> Not, "Good job. Now let's see if you can beat that tomorrow." Not, "You fixed it, but you came to work late." Save these "but"s to talk about another time.

Don't erase your own positive comment!

- Personalize: Name WHO did WHAT

> Not, "Everyone did a great job," but, "Jan, you tested that idea and gave us the data we needed to make a valuable process change."

"Show and Tell" Recognition

What Is "Show and Tell"?

It's when you say to a co-worker, "I heard your idea made this operation safer. Would you show me and tell me how you did it?" Then listen without offering ways to change it. Sometimes *listening* is the best recognition you can give.

And when you want to "show and tell" something you've accomplished, you (or a co-worker) can say, "Please come over here when you have a minute. I've improved something that I'd like to show you."

Labeling a conversation "show and tell" signals that "I want you to know about an improvement I've made and show you how it works." When you make "show and tell" an accepted part of your work routine, you'll start seeing more and more things to recognize.

"Show and Tell" in Everyday Life

You've seen the bumper sticker: "My child is an honor student." The parent who puts it on her car is proud of her son's or daughter's grades; that parent is "showing and telling" her child's achievement with the bumper sticker. Other people will make positive comments to her. She will repeat these comments to her daughter or son, who hears about other people's approval of her or his accomplishment. That family is building a family tradition of pride in achievement. You can build the same at work.

"Show and Tell" on YouTube

Paul Akers started a revolution with his "2 Second Lean" videos on YouTube. His short videos showed simple, everyday job improvements *and* the people who made the improvements. Check them out at http://www.youtube.com/user/fastcaptv.

As baseball giant Yogi Berra said, "You can see a lot by observing."

Think of a time when you've heard an idea from a co-worker that made your work easier or made your product or service better. Using the form that follows, jot it down and then go tell that person that you value it! After you tell the person, give him the note.

Thumbs Up to _____

Your idea of _____

made work easier because

_____

My thanks to you!

Signed: _____

You might just copy this form, complete it, and give it to that co-worker. This will make his or her day! (Be sure to sign it. That will make it extra valuable.)

Appendix VI: Pinch Point Warnings: The Collection

Here are all the pinch points covered in the book—here in one place for you to review and avoid!

Pinch Point Warning #1: Criticizing and blaming will shut down any willingness to try something new.
You: "This process is terrible!"
Co-worker: "Don't blame me. We have to do it this way."

Pinch Point Warning #2: You could "pinch" off your co-workers' flow of ideas with constant criticism. Then they'll stop giving you ideas. Instead, choose ideas to test. Then pick the idea that tests the best.

 **Pinch Point Warning #3:** Keep your graphs and project logs up to date or take them down. Out-of-date graphs become wallpaper and teach everyone to *ignore* posted information.

 **Pinch Point Warning #4:** When you give positive recognition, let it stand alone. Don't follow it with "but." Example: "Noah, you gave us a good idea. But you didn't volunteer to test it." Give your positive recognition and STOP. This will give your recognition time to sink in and have maximum effect. Ask for anything else you need at a *different time.* And **no buts!** "But" erases the positive thing you just said.

 **Pinch Point Warning #5:** When teaching and sharing skills, small steps are the keys to success.

Be careful not to overwhelm your co-worker with too much to learn at one time.

 **Pinch Point Warning #6:** Don't "water the whiners" by listening to them. Listening to them is like watering a weed. Trying to convince them is like watering a weed. It only grows worse. Ignore them and spend time with the people who *want* to make the work easier and better.

Appendix VII: WD-40 Tips: The Collection

WD-40 to Keep Everything Moving Freely

Here are all the WD-40 tips in the book. Come here and review them often, or copy and post them!

Use engagement WD-40: It keeps everything moving freely!

Engagement WD-40 Tip #1

Suggest your idea
<u>and</u> a way to test your idea.

Use engagement WD-40: It keeps everything moving freely!

Engagement WD-40 Tip #2

Write each step of your work on a separate index card or sticky note. This helps you keep the steps separate when you analyze your process.
Then you can ask, "What if … ?"
It also allows you to experiment with rearranging steps later.
Ask, "Would doing the steps in a different sequence make it easier … ?"

Use engagement WD-40:
It keeps everything
moving freely!

Engagement WD-40 Tip #3

Think of what you WANT to happen
(your solution idea) and then *ask* to try out
your idea.
You: "I'd like to re-position the plaster
pitcher to get it out of the walking path.
OK if I try it?"
Co-worker: "OK, give it a try and let me
know how it works.

Use engagement WD-40:
It keeps everything
moving freely!

Engagement WD-40 Tip #4

Ask your co-workers for new ideas to
make the work easier.
Test their ideas. Then recognize them
for their help.

Use engagement WD-40:
It keeps everything
moving freely!

Engagement WD-40 Tip #5

Ask Specific Questions
Be specific when you ask others for their
ideas. Being specific gives them something
concrete to focus on.
Not, "How can we improve?" but
"How can we eliminate these burrs in the
finished metal?"

Use engagement WD-40:
It keeps everything
moving freely!

Engagement WD-40 Tip #6

Graph it!
Post graphs to give you a "moving picture"
of your progress. A picture is
worth a thousand words.

Use engagement WD-40:
It keeps everything
moving freely!

Engagement WD-40 Tip #7

Level 'Em!
Level your ideas to get them "un-stuck."
Level your ideas to create small, concrete
steps that you can DO today.

Use engagement WD-40:
It keeps everything
moving freely!

Engagement WD-40 Tip #8

If your team is arguing about an idea,
stop and:
1. Test the idea
2. Get more facts about what causes
   the problem
3. Go to your customer's workplace
   to SEE how they're using your
   product or service

Use engagement WD-40: It keeps everything moving freely!

Engagement WD-40 Tip #9

Nice is nice. Recognition Points at What People DID.

Some say, "But I always say something nice to everybody." We want and expect our co-workers to be "nice." *Recognition*, however, points out what someone DID that's helpful. Just as you spray WD-40 exactly where it's needed, you "point" your recognition to exactly what your co-worker DID. For example, "You printed the 5S labels for all the parts bins. Looking good."

Use engagement WD-40: It keeps everything moving freely!

Engagement WD-40 Tip #10

Let your co-workers know that you notice and appreciate their help and effort. Make your notice noticed! How?

E.P.T.

 Eye contact

 Point to what they did

 Thumbs Up sign of approval

*Use engagement WD-40:
It keeps everything
moving freely!*

Engagement WD-40 Tip #11:

- For effective training, take your hands off the tool (or keyboard) and step away from the work table. Let your learner do the operation with HER FINGERS. Ask your learner to "talk through it as you do it."
- YOU watch and listen. Recognize your learner for improvement. Correct mistakes and have the learner practice again.

Appendix VIII: Forms

On the following pages are copies of all the forms to make this process clear and easy. Feel free to copy them for use within your organization.

Work process I'd like to make easier: _____	
Solution ideas I'd like to test:	
1.	
2.	
3.	

A customer I would like to visit to see how they use our "stuff" (product or service):	Possible improvements to us and the customers (including making it easier to use our products, less re-work, fewer returns):
	1.
	2.
	3.
	4.
	5.

How to stop disagreeing and start improving			
Possible solution that we don't have agreement on:	Suggestion for performing a test to see if the idea will work:	Data, information, or feedback we can gather from the customer to see if the idea will work:	What we learned from testing or visiting the customer:
_____ _____ _____	_____ _____ _____	_____ _____ _____	_____ _____ _____
	Who will perform this test_____ by _____(date)	Who will visit the customer _____ by _____(date)	

"Here's an idea I'd like to try ..."

| Team Log for _____ (team) | | | | |
| Date _____ Project _____ | | | | |
Idea	Action Step	Volunteer	Target Date	Status

Project _____

Steps to complete the project

Step 6: _____							
Step 5: _____							
Step 4: _____							
Step 3: _____							
Step 2: _____							
Step 1: _____							
Dates:	_____	_____	_____	_____	_____	_____	_____

Project graph measuring: _____(results)

Department: _____

Measurement by numbers or % ___								Goal
	Current level	Week ending	/ Date	/ Date	/ Date	/ Date	/ Date	/ Date

Thumbs Up to _____

Your idea of _____

made work easier because

_____

My thanks you!

Signed: _____

Definitions

brainstorming: a quick way to generate a large number of ideas. Anyone can start brainstorming by asking for ideas on a specific topic and writing down *all* ideas with no judgment or criticism

communication: words, actions, body language, facial expressions, documents, and signs that send messages to other people

co-workers: everyone we work with in our organizations (up, down, and sideways)

culture: the actions and words in an organization for which people show approval or disapproval; often informal and not written down—"the way we do things around here"

engage: to gain and hold attention and interest; to participate

feedback: information on performance that helps someone know how to improve

goal: the measurable result we want to achieve

graph: data posted visually showing current level, goal, and actual performance. Dots, lines, or bars show a trend over a time period

leveling: the process to determine whether ideas can be implemented or tested right away (Level 1), need approvals (Level 2), or can only be implemented or tested with more information (Level 3)

listen: understand another person's message before offering a response (could you pass a quiz on what the person said?)

motivate: to inspire a person to *want* to do something

positive recognition: acknowledging a person for his or her actions, causing him or her to want to repeat those actions

pull method: in lean process, wait for a customer order (internal or external) before producing a product or service

push method: in lean process, to create a product for "stock" (hoping a customer will order it later)

recognition: see positive recognition

show and tell: to ask someone to show the improvement they've made and tell how they did it; a form of recognition

sub-goals: small, incremental improvements leading to a final goal

time goal: the target date to complete an action step

Resources

Books

How to Engage, Involve, and Motivate Employees: Building a Culture of Lean Leadership and Two-Way Communication, by Janis Allen and Michael McCarthy (CRC Press, 2017). Companion to this book, *Ready? Set? Engage!* The 5-Step Method for supervisors, managers, and leaders to help employees get started with projects and give support to help them succeed.

Sustain Your Gains: The People Side of Lean-Six Sigma, by Michael McCarthy (Performance Management Publications, 2011). Accelerate improvement and sustain your gains from Lean and Six Sigma. This book shows how to make improvements into new habits that sustain. How to stop losing your hard-won Lean and Six Sigma gains.

You Made My Day: Creating Co-Worker Recognition and Relationships, by Janis Allen and Michael McCarthy (Performance Leadership Publications, 2005). Build teamwork and performance by showing employees, supervisors, and managers when and how to give positive recognition. Build a more positive culture.

5S Made Easy: A Step-by-Step Guide to Implementing and Sustaining Your 5S Program, by David Visco (CRC Press, 2015). In-depth guidance on how to implement and sustain each of the 5S pillars—sort, set in order, shine, standardize, and sustain. "Before" and "after" pictures of real-world 5S solutions and useful forms.

2 Second Lean (How to Grow People and Build a Fun Lean Culture at Work and at Home), by Paul A. Akers (Fastcap Press, 2014). *2 Second Lean* will flip your world right-side up. It's a practical way to improve your life every day by making simple two-second improvements. Join author, business expert, radio show host, and international speaker, Paul A. Akers, as he takes you on a LEAN journey that will transform every aspect your life … from your home to the office.

Bringing out the Best in People, by Aubrey C. Daniels (Performance Management Publications, 2000). How to transform work into something people are willing, ready, and even eager to do. www.aubreydaniels.com

Audio

Do's and Don'ts for Delivering Recognition (and Receiving It) for Teams, Co-Workers, and Supervisors (one-hour CD), by Janis Allen interviewed by Michael McCarthy (Performance Leadership Publications, 2013). Practical tips for giving positive recognition that doesn't cost a dime. How to overcome skepticism of your receivers. How to prevent blunders and deal effectively with recognition resistors.

Webinars (customized for your organization)

Sustain Your Gains: Training for quality managers, CI professionals, supervisors, and managers to sustain your gains from Lean-Six Sigma using PBM (Process Behavior Maintenance). Three one-hour sessions spaced one to two weeks apart, with on-the-job practice and assignments, for up to 12 participants. Contact: mikemccarthy@sustainleangains.com

Ready? Set? Engage! Training helps accelerate your effective use of the tools in this book. Three 45-minute sessions delivered live to your supervisors or team leaders, either in person or via webinar. Spaced one week apart with action assignments in between. Don't just get trained, get started! To learn how to make this work for you, contact mikemccarthy@sustainleangains.com.

Culture

Winning Ways to a Positive Culture, deck of 52 playing cards to make learning and doing fun. Grouped in four "suites" or categories: Recognition, Teamwork, Positive Culture, and Customer Service, 52 specific ideas you can implement in your workplace immediately for culture change you can see and hear. Contact: janisallen@janisallen.com

Websites

www.sustainleangains.com
www.janisallen.com
www.the5Sstore.com

Ready? Set? Engage! Trainer Certification

Are you a team leader, training manager, continuous improvement coordinator, safety supervisor, or human resources manager? If so, you may want to be certified to conduct RSE (Ready? Set? Engage!) training. Contact: mikemccarthy@sustainleangains.com

Index